THEMATIC UNIT
Planets

Written By Jennifer Overend Prior, M.Ed.

Teacher Created Materials, Inc.
6421 Industry Way
Westminster, CA 92683
www.teachercreated.com

©2001 *Teacher Created Materials, Inc.*
Made in U.S.A.

ISBN-0-7439-3076-2

Illustrated by
Ken Tunell

Edited by
Karen Tam Froloff

Cover Art by
Denice Adorno

Table of Contents

Introduction

Planets is a captivating, comprehensive thematic unit. Its 80 exciting pages are filled with a wide variety of lesson ideas designed for use with primary-aged students. At its core are two high quality student's literature selections, *Louis and the Night Sky* and *Postcards from Pluto*. For these books, activities are included which set the stage for reading, encourage enjoyment of the book, and extend the concepts learned. In addition, the theme is connected to the curriculum with activities in language arts (including daily writing suggestions), math, science, social studies, art, music, and movement. Many of these activities encourage cooperative learning. Suggestions and patterns for bulletin boards and unit management tools are additional time savers for the busy teacher. Furthermore, directions for student-created Big Books and culminating activities are included, which allow students to apply their new-found knowledge.

This thematic unit includes the following:

❏ **literature selections**—summaries of two children's books with related lessons (complete with reproducible pages) that cross the curriculum

❏ **poetry**—suggested selections

❏ **planning guides**—suggestions for sequencing lessons each day of the unit

❏ **writing ideas**—daily suggestions as well as writing activities across the curriculum, including a Big Book

❏ **bulletin board ideas**—suggestions and plans for student-created and/or interactive bulletin boards

❏ **curriculum connections**—in language arts, math, science, art, music, and movement

❏ **group projects**—activities that foster cooperative learning

❏ **a culminating activity**—which requires students to synthesize their learning to produce a product or engage in an activity that can be shared with others

---

To keep this valuable resource intact so that it can be used year after year, you may wish to punch holes in the pages and store them in a three-ring binder.

Introduction (cont.)

Why a Balanced Approach?

The strength of a balanced language approach is that it involves students in using all modes of communication—reading, writing, listening, illustrating, and doing. Communication skills are interconnected and integrated into lessons that emphasize the whole of language. Implicit in this approach is the knowledge that every whole—including individual words—is composed of parts, and directed study of those parts can help a student to master the whole. Experience and research tell us that regular attention to phonics, other word attack skills, spelling, etc., develops reading mastery, thereby fulfilling the unity of the whole language experience. The student is thus led to read, write, spell, speak, and listen more confidently.

Why Thematic Planning?

One very useful tool for implementing an integrated language program is thematic planning. By choosing a theme with a correlating literature selection for a unit of study, a teacher can plan activities throughout the day that lead to a cohesive, in-depth study of the topic. Students will be practicing and applying their skills in meaningful context. Consequently, they tend to learn and retain more.

Why Cooperative Learning?

Besides academic skills and content, students need to learn social skills. No longer can this area of development be taken for granted. Students must learn to work cooperatively in groups in order to function well in modern society. Group activities should be a regular part of school life and teachers should consciously include social objectives as well as academic objectives in their planning.

Why Big Books?

An excellent cooperative, whole language activity is the production of Big Books. Groups of students, or the whole class, can apply their language skills, context knowledge, and creativity to produce a Big Book that becomes a part of the classroom library to be read and reread. These books make excellent culminating projects for sharing beyond the classroom with parents, librarians, other classes, etc.

Why Journals?

Each day students should have the opportunity to write in a journal. They may respond to a book or an event in history, write about a personal experience, or answer a general "question of the day" posed by the teacher. The cumulative journal provides an excellent means of documenting the student's writing progress.

Louis and the Night Sky

by Nicola Morgan

Summary

Louis doesn't want to go to sleep. He wishes he could live on a planet where it is always day. He decides to go on a journey through the solar system, in search of the perfect planet. Louis travels past all of the planets, but can't find a place to live until he sees a blue marble twinkling in space. As he journeys to this friendly planet, he realizes that Earth is the best home after all.

The outline below is a suggested plan for using the various activities that are presented in this unit.

Sample Plan

Lesson I

- Create a KWL chart (page 6, Setting the Stage, #2).
- Read *Louis and the Night Sky.*
- Introduce The Planetarium (page 63).
- Complete a Daily Writing Activity (pages 20 and 21).
- Make a Milky Way Galaxy art project (page 7, Extending the Book, #1).
- Look at the planet pictures on a Web site (page 7, Extending the Book, #2).

Lesson II

- Reread *Louis and the Night Sky.* Have the students retell the story using verbal sequencing.
- Complete Story Sequencing (page 9).
- Complete Order the Planets (page 25).
- Use the Research Outline to research a planet (page 7, Extending the Book, #3 and #4).
- Make a Miniature Solar System (page 51).

Lesson III

- Reread *Louis and the Night Sky.* Have students describe the planets as they listen (page 6, Enjoying the Book, #1).
- Recite a planetary poem (page 7, Extending the Book, #5).
- Complete a Daily Writing Activity (pages 20 and 21).
- Complete Riddle Math (page 26).
- Make a Solar System Booklet (page 7, Extending the Book, #6).
- Sing a Space Song (page 56).

Lesson IV

- Read another planet book (see Bibliography, pages 77 and 78).
- Recite a planetary poem (page 7, Extending the Book, #5).
- Complete a Daily Writing Activity (pages 20 and 21).
- Participate in a planet experiment (page 37).
- Make a shadow clock (pages 38 and 39).
- Learn about the first moon landing and make a rocket booklet and moon rocks (pages 40–42).
- Complete Space Journey Application (page 7, Extending the Book, #7).
- Sing another Space Song (page 56).
- Make a Milky Way Cookie (page 57).

Lesson V

- Recite a planetary poem (page 7, Extending the Book, #5).
- Complete a Daily Writing Activity (pages 20 and 21).
- Learn about the *Voyager* Space Probes (page 43).
- Make a *Voyager* Mini-Booklet (pages 44 and 45).
- Visit another Web site (page 7, Extending the Book, #2).

Overview of Activities

Setting the Stage

1. Set the stage for your unit about planets by creating Our Sensational Solar System bulletin board on page 62. Invite students to study the bulletin board and to pronounce the names of the planets.

2. Make a KWL chart with your students, asking them to tell things they know about planets, things they want to know, and the things they learn throughout the unit.

Know	Want to Know	Learned

3. There are many new words that students will encounter during this unit, such as *rotate*, *orbit*, *asteroid*, *galaxy*, *crater*, and *gravity*. Make a list of these words as they are encountered and then continue reading and doing research to find the meaning of these words. Be sure to add definitions to the list as they are found.

4. Motivate students to investigate space and the solar system by setting up a planetarium corner in the room. See pages 63–64 for suggestions.

Enjoying the Book

1. Draw the students' attention to the descriptive words used in *Louis and the Night Sky*. Draw particular attention to the words used to describe the planets. Then have the students listen to the story again and complete Describing the Planets on page 10.

2. Ask your students if they have ever had trouble sleeping like Louis. Invite them to give suggestions to Louis that might help him to sleep.

3. Why can't Louis sleep? Is he afraid of the dark? Ask the students if they have ever been afraid of the dark. Make a class bar graph showing the students' responses.

4. Engage students in a discussion, asking the following questions:

   - Why does Louis want to live on a planet that is always light?

   - If a person could go on a trip like Louis, what would he or she really need in order to travel through space?

   - Is there a planet that is always light?

5. Many of the illustrations in the book show Louis sitting on, standing on, or flying past a planet. Have each student draw a picture of himself or herself on or flying past a favorite planet.

6. Review *Louis and the Night Sky* with the students. Have them complete the sequencing activity on page 9 and share their responses.

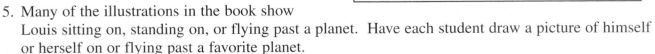

Overview of Activities *(cont.)*

Extending the Book

1. Explain to students that our solar system is a very small part of a galaxy called the Milky Way. This galaxy has many other solar systems in it. Discuss the facts below and then have each student make the Milky Way Galaxy art project on page 50.

   - The Milky Way is a large group of stars, called a galaxy.

   - Our solar system is in the Milky Way Galaxy.

   - From a distance, a galaxy looks like a hazy circle or swirling light.

   - The hazy look comes from the light of so many stars.

   - It is possible to see the Milky Way on clear, moonless nights. It looks like a bright band across the sky.

   - The Milky Way Galaxy contains billions of stars. There are two kinds of stars—brilliant, blue stars and giant, red stars.

   - Just like the Earth rotates, our galaxy rotates, too. It takes about 200 million years for the galaxy to rotate one time.

2. Enhance your planets unit by accessing Web sites with actual photographs of the planets. You'll find a variety of Web sites on page 74. The URL address for these sites can be found on TCM's Web site, where addresses can be updated. (See www.teachercreated.com/books/3076)

3. Encourage students to do their own planet research using the Research Outline on page 36. Have each student select a planet to research, locate resource books about the planet, and complete the outline. Extend the activity by having each student use the information gathered on the outline to write a research report. If desired, have the students write their reports on the Star Stationery on page 69.

4. Before engaging in planet research, brainstorm a list of questions the students have about the solar system or the planets. This will help students to formulate a direction for their research.

5. Give students the opportunity to memorize the planetary poems on pages 18 and 19. This can be done easily by repeating a poem several times. Then say each line of the poem, asking the students to repeat it.

6. To help students learn more about the planets, have them make the Solar System Booklet on pages 30–35. To assemble the booklet, have each student cut on the dashed lines and then stack the pages in order. Then staple the booklet along the left edge to form the spine. Encourage students to color the illustrations and read the information with classmates. Have students take their booklets home to read and discuss with family members.

Overview of Activities *(cont.)*

Extending the Book *(cont.)*

7. After learning about astronauts and space discoveries, students may be interested in space travel. Have each student complete the Space Journey Application on page 24, telling why he or she would like to travel in space.

8. As a homework assignment, have a family member spread a blanket on the ground and star-gaze on a moonless night. Ask the family member to have the student look for star formations (constellations), shooting stars, the Milky Way, and larger bright "stars" which could be planets. Encourage students to share their star-gazing experiences with the class.

9. Explain to the students that telescopes are used by astronomers to see stars, planets, and other objects in the solar system. Telescopes have high-powered lenses that make the objects appear much closer than they really are. It is possible, however, to see many of the planets with the naked eye or by simply using a good pair of binoculars. As the students' curiosity with planets and stars builds, they may want to use binoculars or telescopes to view stars and planets. Be sure to warn them, however, that even though they may be interested in the sun, they must never look directly at it. Extend students' knowledge by discussing the *Voyager* space probes (page 43).

10. Help your students learn facts about some *Voyager* discoveries by creating mini-booklets to read and share with others. Duplicate the mini-booklet on pages 44 and 45. Have each student color, cut out, and assemble the pages. Staple the booklet at the top. Review the comprehension questions on the final pages of the booklet with the students. Then, instruct them to read the booklet and underline the correct answers. Next, read the story together in class. As you review the questions and what has been underlined in the booklet, have the students write their answers on the comprehension pages.

Story Sequencing

Look at the illustrations and read the six sentences. Cut apart the illustrations and glue them onto a new piece of paper in the correct story order.

Louis couldn't fall asleep.

Louis traveled past Pluto.

Louis looked at the night sky.

He saw a twinkling planet in the sky.

He traveled past Venus.

Louis came home and went to sleep.

Describing the Planets

Listen to your teacher read the story, *Louis and the Night Sky* by Nicola Morgan. Complete the page.

1. Which planet is dry and dusty? _____

2. Which planet is dark and gloomy? _____

3. Which planet is small and red? _____

4. Describe Jupiter. _____

   _____

5. Describe Saturn. _____

   _____

6. Which planet is sea-green? _____

7. Which planet is covered with ice? _____

8. Describe Pluto. _____

   _____

Draw a picture of Louis traveling through space.

Postcards from Pluto

by Loreen Leedy

Summary

In this brightly illustrated book, a group of school students go on a Space Tour Journey through the solar system with Dr. Quaser. As the students learn factual information about the planets and the solar system, they write postcards to their friends and family members, sharing their knowledge.

The outline below is a suggested plan for using the various activities that are presented in this unit.

Sample Plan

Lesson I
- Read *Postcards from Pluto* by Loreen Leedy.
- Use the Puppet Props to act out the story (page 12, Enjoying the Book, #1).
- Complete a Daily Writing Activity (pages 20 and 21).
- Complete What's in a Name? (page 12, Enjoying the Book, #2).
- Make a Magnetosphere art project (page 52).
- Sing a Space Song (page 56).
- Play a game (page 58).
- Creating invitations and programs for the Solar System Culmination (page 13, Extending the Book, #1).
- Visit a planet Web site (page 74).

Lesson II
- Reread *Postcards from Pluto*.
- Write a postcard to a family member (page 12, Enjoying the Book, #3).
- Recite a Planetary Poem (pages 18 and 19).
- Complete a Daily Writing Activity (pages 20 and 21).
- Make a Big Book (page 13, Extending the Book, #2).
- Complete Celestial Similes (page 23).
- Complete Planet Chart (page 13, Extending the Book, #3).
- Participate in a space experiment (page 37).
- Complete a planet Web Site Activity Sheet (page 13, Extending the Book, #4).

Lesson III
- Read another planet book (Bibliography, pages 77 and 78).
- Complete Celestial Crossword (page 13, Enjoying the Book, #7).
- Recite a planetary poem (pages 18 and 19).

- Complete Hours in a Day (page 13, Extending the Book, #5).
- Make Stars in a Box (pages 53 and 54).
- Sing a Space Song (page 56).
- Make Solar System Cookies (page 57).

Lesson IV
- Read another planet book.
- Recite a planetary poem.
- Complete a Daily Writing Activity (pages 20 and 21).
- Give able students a challenge by completing Happy Birthday to You! (page 13, Extending the Book, #6).
- Participate in another space experiment (page 37).
- Complete How Much Do You Weigh? (page 14, Extending the Book, #7).
- Make a Space Creature Pencil Can (page 55).
- Play a game (page 58).
- Visit a planet Web site (page 74).
- Begin the Solar System Culmination (page 60).

Lesson V
- Read another planet book.
- Recite a planetary poem (pages 18 and 19).
- Complete a Daily Writing Activity (pages 20 and 21).
- Learn about the planet Pluto (page 14, Extending the Book, #8).
- Learn about constellations (page 14, Extending the Book, #9).
- Play Race to the Sun (page 14, Extending the Book, #10).
- Complete Are You a Planet Expert? (page 14, Extending the Book, #11).
- Complete the Solar System Culmination (page 60).

Overview of Activities

Setting the Stage

1. Create the Stellar Stories bulletin board (page 62) to display your students' writing projects.

2. Engage the students in a discussion about writing letters and postcards to friends and family members. Ask them if they have ever written postcards or had some mailed to them.

Enjoying the Book

1. Duplicate, color, cut out, and glue the props on page 15 to tagboard. If desired, laminate the props for durability. Staple or glue a craft stick to the bottom of each shape. Use the props to retell the story. (You can also make planet props in the same manner using the clip art on pages 70–72.)

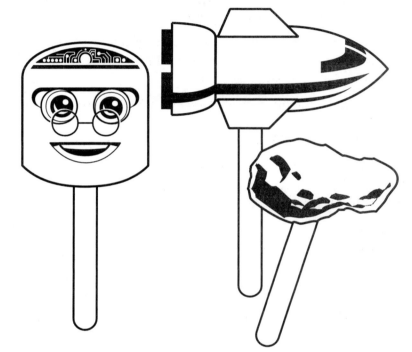

2. Ask the students if anyone they know uses a nickname for them. Explain that nicknames usually describe something about a person. Some planets have nicknames, too. Have each student complete What's in a Name? (page 22) to match the planets to their nicknames.

3. After reading the story, *Postcards from Pluto*, have each student write a postcard (page 16) to a family member telling about new information learned about a planet. Show the students how to address their postcards and even encourage them to make space illustrations on their stamps.

4. Continue practice with letter-writing skills by having each student write a letter to Dr. Quaser of *Postcards from Pluto*. Have each student include specific facts he or she learned from the book.

5. Have some fun with rebus writing. In the story, *Postcards from Pluto*, the students use pictures in place of some of the words. Invite your students to write letters or stories of their own, substituting some of the words with drawings.

6. Generate creativity by having each student create a large postcard stamp with a planetary illustration. Allow the students to skim planet books with photos (see Bibliography on pages 77 and 78) or view photos at Internet Web sites (page 74) for inspiration and ideas for their designs.

7. The use of figurative language can make writing more creative, interesting, and more understandable. Introduce similes to the class by providing examples and encouraging students to create their own to share. Place a chart in the room with several good examples of similes. Then, have students complete page 23 and share their responses.

12

Overview of Activities *(cont.)*

7. Now that your students have learned many things about the planets and the solar system, it's time to put that knowledge to the test with Celestial Crossword on page 17. Have the students use *Postcards from Pluto* and other informational books to help with the puzzle's completion.

Extending the Book

1. With the Solar System Culmination only a few days away, it's time to start preparing the invitations and programs (page 61). Also, ask the students to start thinking about the information they would like to share with their guests when they arrive.

2. Making a Big Book is a great way to show the knowledge your students have gained throughout the unit. See page 65 for detailed instructions for creating a class or group Big Book. The completed project is a great display piece for parents and administrators.

3. There is much to learn about the characteristics of each of the planets. Completing the Planet Chart on page 27 will help the students to compare and contrast the planets, identifying which have moons, life, rings, and clouds and which ones are inner or outer planets.

4. The Space Place is a must-see Web site with lots of student-friendly activities and information. Duplicate page 76 for each student and allow time at and away from the computer to complete the projects given at this motivational site.

5. Engage students in a discussion about the length of a day on Earth. Be sure to demonstrate the Earth's rotation by participating in What Makes a Day? on page 37. Explain to the students that each planet rotates at a different speed and share that Venus even rotates in the opposite direction of the other planets. Some planets have long days and some have short days. Then have each student complete Hours in a Day on page 28.

6. Do you have students who need an added challenge? Happy Birthday to You! on page 29 is not for everyone. Completing this page involves using the information on a chart and comparing the length of each planet's year to answer questions about having birthdays in each place.

Overview of Activities *(cont.)*

Extending the Book *(cont.)*

7. Lead your students in a discussion about gravity. Explain that gravity is a force that gives us weight. It is what keeps us on the ground rather than floating in the air. Each planet has a different gravitational force, so on some planets a person would weigh more or less than he or she does on Earth. Completing How Much Do You Weigh? on page 46 will help your students determine which planets have more or less gravity than Earth. Also, don't miss visiting the Your Weight on Other Worlds Web site (page 74) where a student can type in his or her weight and immediately see how much he or she would weigh on each of the planets and their moons.

8. There have been many debates about the classification of Pluto. Is it really a planet or is it an asteroid? Share the information from Is Pluto a Planet? on page 47 and then have students participate in one or all of the suggested activities.

9. Discuss with your students the fact that stars stay in approximately the same place from day to day. In fact, there are star formations, called constellations, that are easy to recognize in the night sky. By completing It's in the Stars on page 48, your students will become familiar with the four different constellations of Orion, the Big Dipper, Cassiopeia, and Leo. The final project results in a star-studded display.

10. Students will gather even more fascinating information by playing Race to the Sun. To prepare the game, duplicate and color the game board on page 49. Laminate it for durability or staple it to a sheet of tagboard. Duplicate page 68. The fact cards are stacked and placed facedown beside the game board. Use simple game pieces, such as coins, or get creative and press marbles into small portions of clay. This game is purely informative, so even solar system beginners will have no trouble playing and winning.

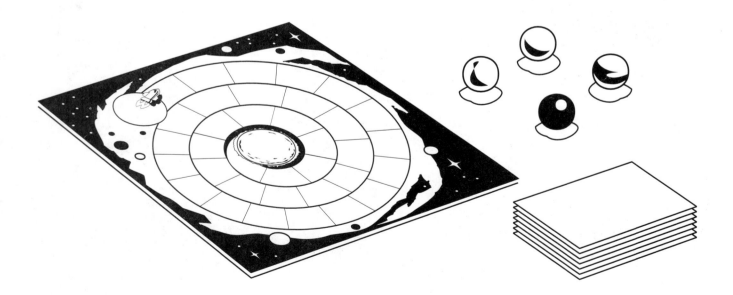

11. Test your students' knowledge at the end of the unit by having them complete Are You a Planet Expert? on page 59.

Puppet Props

See page 12, Enjoying the Book, #1 for suggested use.

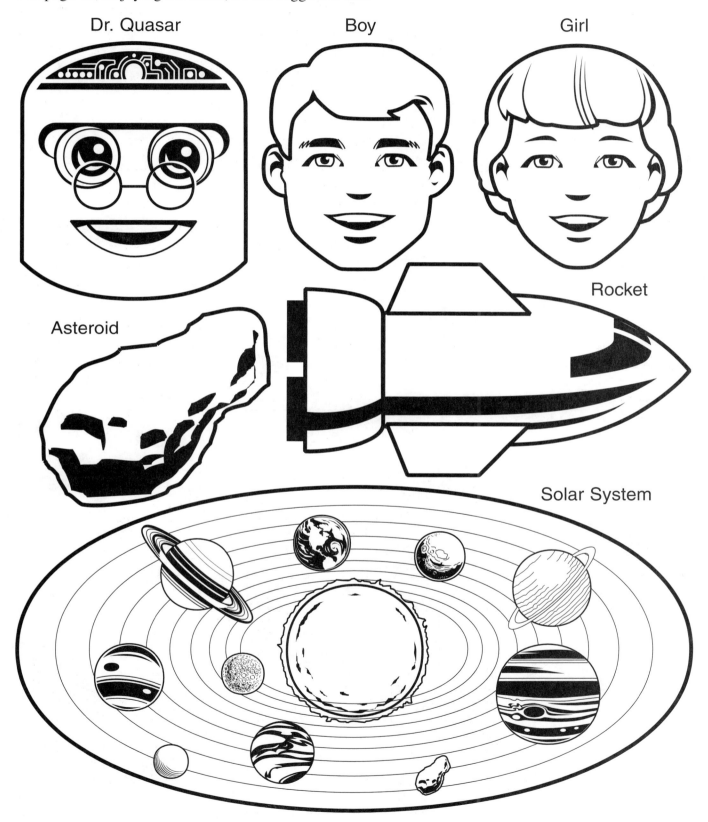

Dr. Quasar

Boy

Girl

Rocket

Asteroid

Solar System

Postcard Pattern

Celestial Crossword

Complete the puzzle, using the word bank below.

Word Bank

orbit	sun	star	Saturn
Neptune	Uranus	Mars	moon
planets	galaxy	Mercury	rotate
Venus	Earth	Jupiter	Pluto

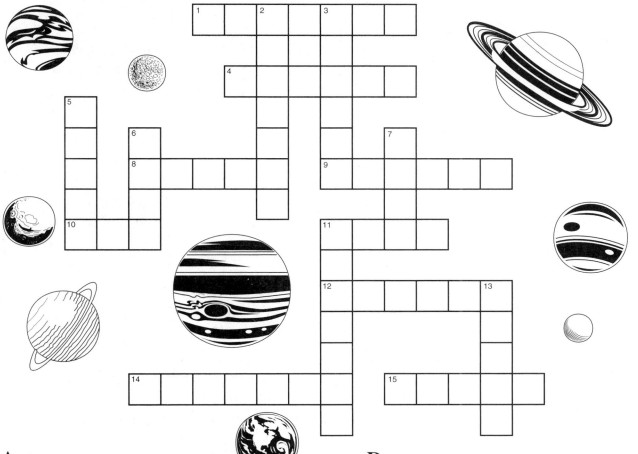

Across

1. the planet with blue clouds
4. a big group of stars
8. a path around something
9. the planet known for its many rings
10. The planets revolve around this star.
11. the red planet
12. to turn around and around
14. the planet with the Great Red Spot
15. the planet farthest away from the sun

Down

2. Nine of them are in our solar system.
3. the planet that is tilted
5. the twin planet of Earth
6. an object in orbit around a planet
7. a large fiery mass in space
11. the closest planet to the sun
13. the only planet with life

Planetary Poetry

Mercury

Do you know which planet sits the closest to our star?
It's very hard to see this place, if Earth is where you are.
How hot and dry and sun-baked, and hardly any air.
Without a drop of water, no life can be found there.

Venus

Clouds of water vapor surround this lonely place.
Lightning storms and thunder, all through the sky
    they race.
Temperatures in winter, and summer, spring, and fall,
Are scorching hot the year 'round on this planetary
    ball.

Earth

Of all the planets that I know, this one's the best of all,
With sunny days and air to breathe, and trees that grow so tall.
On starry nights, I gaze above and count the falling stars,
And think about this planet, Earth, how beautiful you are!

Mars

This little planet, small and red, how interesting are
    you.
Volcanoes, canyons, channels, wow, I see you have
    them, too!
You have two moons, our neighbor Mars, and
    seasons through the year.
But somehow I don't think I'll be vacationing up there.

Jupiter

The largest planet of the nine, it's often called the
    "King."
A giant among planets, and like Saturn it has rings.
With four large moons, and many small, it travels
    'round the sun.
A planet of this magnitude, I'm glad there's only one!

Planetary Poetry *(cont.)*

Saturn

This giant planet, number six, is known for
  many things,
But most of all, I'm sure you know, it's noted
  for those rings.
Its rings are made of rock and dust, and even
  bits of ice.
I may not call this planet home, but still I think
  it's nice.

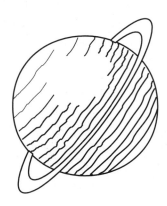

Uranus

Where in all the universe, will you ever really see,
A planet tilted on its side, it is a mystery.
This planet has a few small rings and five large
  moons, on my!
As you can see, it's quite a sight, this planet in the
  sky.

Neptune

Far away, so far away, this planet glows so blue,
Take a closer look and see a ring, or maybe two.
Its atmosphere is cloudy; it travels all about.
Planet eight's mysterious, of that I have no doubt.

Pluto

Traveling oh so many years to circle 'round the sun,
This distant tiny Pluto, must be a lonely one.
Our ninth and farthest planet is blanketed with ice;
I think a trip to Pluto would not be very nice!

Daily Writing Activities

Postcards from Space

Ask the students to imagine that they are traveling in outer space. What would they tell their families about the experience? Then duplicate the postcard pattern on page 16 and distribute one to each student. Have the student write, illustrate, and address a postcard, including interesting information about planets and the solar system.

Journal Writing

To inspire students' journal writing, display one of the following questions or topics daily:

- Imagine that you are an astronaut. Describe an experience in space.
- Write about your favorite planet.
- How do you think it would feel to be weightless?
- Do you think there is life on other planets?
- Have you ever looked at the night sky? Write about what you have seen.
- Do you think it would be scary to travel in space? Why or why not?
- If people could live on another planet, would you want to move there? Write about it.
- Write about what scientists and astronauts learn from studying outer space.

Draw and Write

- Draw a picture of your favorite planet. Write three facts you know about it.
- Draw a picture of yourself as an astronaut. Write about what you would like to see in space.
- Draw a picture of the solar system. Write each planet's name below it.

Would You Rather . . .

- Would you rather look at space from Earth or take a trip in a spaceship?
- Would you rather take a trip with an alien or have an alien join you at home for dinner?
- Would you rather walk on the moon or see Saturn from a spaceship?
- Would you rather visit Mars or Neptune?
- Would you rather be an astronaut or an astronomer?
- Would you rather look through a telescope or a microscope?
- Would you rather sleep outside under the stars or travel through the stars?
- Would you rather learn new things about Jupiter or Mars?

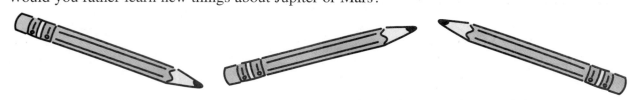

Daily Writing Activities *(cont.)*

Space Riddles

What planet is large, orange and red, and has a large spot on it? It's Jupiter. Have your students use information learned to write riddles about planets or other space objects. Each student writes three clues on a card and writes the answer on the back. Then have the students exchange riddle cards to solve.

Acrostic Poems

Have your students create acrostic poems. Begin by creating one as a class. Write the name of a planet or other space object vertically on chart paper. For each letter of the word, write an adjective to describe the word. Invite the students to contribute to the poem. When finished, brainstorm different subjects that could be used to create individual acrostics. Allow the students to create their own acrostic poems and add illustrations to accompany them.

Shape Poems

Students can easily create their own shape poems. Have each student select a space-related topic or object and then write a rhyming or free verse poem about it. The student then draws a simple outline of the object and then writes the poem along the outline to create the complete shape poem.

Adjective Webs

Make a group adjective web for each of the planets. Begin by reading interesting facts and allowing your students to view photographs of one of the planets. Invite questions and discussion. Then create a web, encouraging students to use descriptive words.

Spacey Stories

Students will enjoy writing crazy space stories with this activity. Begin by duplicating pages 66 and 67 (each page on a different color paper). Cut apart the cards and place each set in its own cup or bag. A student can be inspired to write by selecting one card from each set and putting them together to make a story title. (The student may adapt the words in the title or select different cards to find an innovative title.)

Invite students to share these writings with one another. Divide them into small groups of three or four. Ask each student to choose one piece of writing to bring to his or her sharing group. The students take turns reading their stories, poems, riddles, or other writing. Encourage the groups to ask questions or to make comments on what has been shared.

What's in a Name?

Do you have a nickname? People and pets are often given nicknames that describe them. Some of the planets have nicknames, too.

Read each planet description and cut and paste the nicknames above its illustration and description.

 1. Jupiter is the largest planet. It is about as big as a small star. It is much, much larger than Earth.	2. Mars is known for its color. The dirt on Mars is a reddish color.
 3. Venus is very much like Earth. The two planets are alike. Venus is also almost the same size as Earth.	4. From space, Earth looks like a blue ball. Many people think it looks like a marble.
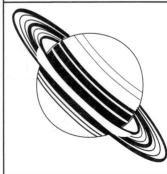 5. Saturn is known for its rings. Other planets have rings, too, but Saturn's rings are very easy to see.	6. Pluto has a large moon. The moon is almost the same size as Pluto. Scientists say that they look like two planets together.

Nicknames:

The Double Planet	Earth's Twin	The Ringed Planet
The Red Planet	The Big Blue Marble	The King of Planets

Celestial Similes

A *simile* compares two different things using *like* or *as*. The following sentence is an example of a simile: The night air was as cold as ice. Can you imagine how cold the air must be? Write your own words or phrases to complete these similes.

1. Jupiter looks as big as _____ .

2. Neptune is as blue as _____ .

3. Mercury is as small as _____ .

4. Venus is as hot as _____ .

5. Mars is as red as _____ .

6. Pluto is as cold as _____ .

7. Earth is as colorful as_____ .

8. Saturn is as _____ as _____ .

9. Uranus is as _____ as _____ .

10. Earth is as _____ as _____ .

11. Jupiter is as _____ as _____ .

12. Venus is as _____ as _____ .

13. Mars is as _____ as _____ .

14. The sun is as _____ as _____ .

Space Journey Application

How would you like to go into space on a spaceship? Pretend that you are applying for a job on a spaceship. Write about the reasons why you should be chosen for this exciting journey.

Name: _____

Age: _____

Grade: _____

Describe yourself. _____

_____

_____

_____

_____

Why do you want to travel into space?

_____

_____

_____

_____

What would you like to learn about space?

_____

_____

_____

_____

Explain how a journey into space would change your life.

_____

_____

_____

_____

Order the Planets

Cut out the boxes and place them in order. Then paste the boxes under or above the planets they name. Draw a line from each box to its planet.

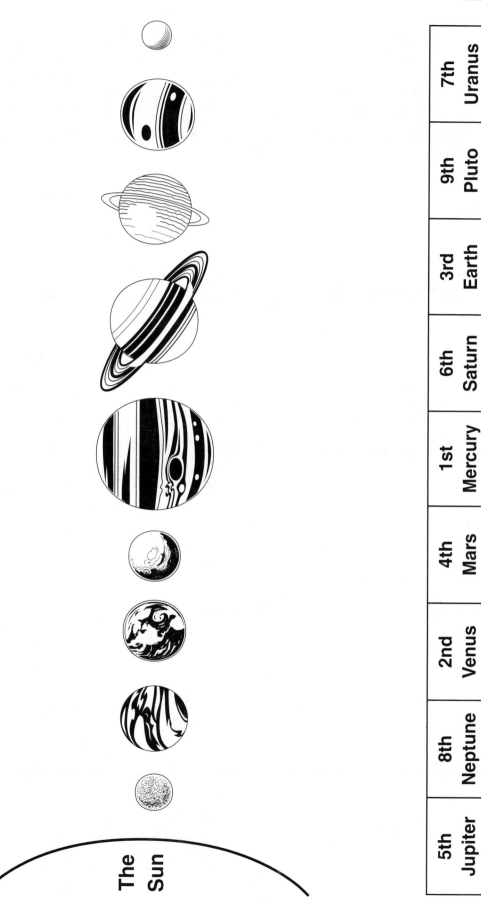

The Sun

5th Jupiter	8th Neptune	2nd Venus	4th Mars	1st Mercury	6th Saturn	3rd Earth	9th Pluto	7th Uranus

Riddle Math

Cut and paste the answer boxes from the bottom of the page into the correct sentences. Use the letters to solve the riddles.

Which planet's name sounds like a song?

___ ___ ___ ___ ___ ___ ___
3   4   2   1   5   7   6

5 − 3 = [   ]   7 − 1 = [   ]   7 − 4 = [   ]

9 − 4 = [   ]   10 − 6 = [   ]   10 − 3 = [   ]   9 − 8 = [   ]

Which planet's name is a cartoon character?

___ ___ ___ ___ ___
13   18   14   16   11

7 + 6 = [   ]   9 + 9 = [   ]

8 + 8 = [   ]   6 + 8 = [   ]   5 + 6 = [   ]

6	1	4	3	7	2
E	T	E	N	N	P
5	14	16	13	18	11
U	U	T	P	L	O

26

Planet Chart

Use the chart to answer the questions.

Planet	Has moons	Has life	Has rings	Inner planet	Outer planet
Mercury				X	
Venus				X	
Earth	X	X		X	
Mars	X			X	
Jupiter	X		X		X
Saturn	X		X		X
Uranus	X		X		X
Neptune	X		X		X
Pluto	X				X

1. Which planets have moons?_____

2. Which planet has life? _____

3. Which planets have rings? _____

4. Name the inner planets. _____

5. Name the outer planets. _____

Hours in a Day

On Earth, a day lasts 24 hours because that's how long it takes our planet to rotate one time. Some planets have short days. Some planets have very long days. Use the chart below to answer the questions.

How Long is the Day?
(In Earth hours and days)

Planet	Day	Planet	Day
Mercury	59 days	Saturn	10½ hours
Venus	243 days	Uranus	17 hours
Earth	24 hours	Neptune	16 hours
Mars	24½ hours	Pluto	6 days
Jupiter	10 hours		

1. Which planet has the shortest day?

   _____

2. Which planet has the longest day?

   _____

3. Which planet has a day nearest in length to Earth's day?

   _____

4. Is a day on Venus longer or shorter than a day on Earth?

   _____

5. Is a day on Pluto longer or shorter than a day on Jupiter?

   _____

6. Which of the inner planets has the shortest day?

   _____

Happy Birthday to You!

A year on Earth is 365 days long. That's the number of days it takes our planet to orbit the sun. Some planets have short years. Some planets have long years. Answer these questions and find out how old you would be on different planets.

How Long is a Year?

Planet	In Earth Days	Planet	In Earth Years
Mercury	88	Jupiter	12
Venus	225	Saturn	30
Earth	365	Uranus	84
Mars	687	Neptune	165
		Pluto	248

1. A year on Mercury is 88 days. About how old would you be if you lived on Mercury? (Hint: Multiply your age by 4.) _____

2. A year on Neptune is 165 Earth years. How many Earth years would you need to live in order to be two years old on Neptune? _____

3. A year on Pluto is 248 Earth years. How many Earth years would you need to live in order to be three years old on Pluto? _____

4. A year on Jupiter takes 12 Earth years. If you had two birthdays on Jupiter, how old would you be on Earth?_____

5. A year on Uranus is 84 Earth years. If you had four birthdays on Uranus, how old would you be on Earth?_____

6. Would you be older if you lived on Saturn or on Mars?_____

7. Which two planets have shorter years than Earth? _____

Solar System Booklet

My Book
of the
Solar System

Name: _____

①

Our Solar System

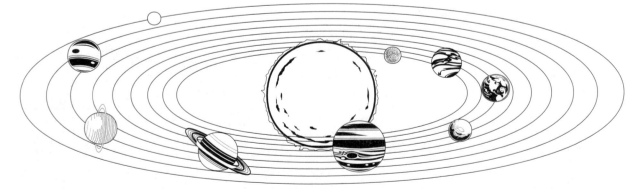

Our solar system has nine planets. The inner planets are Mercury, Venus, Earth, and Mars. The outer planets are Jupiter, Saturn, Uranus, Neptune, and Pluto. We live on the planet Earth. All of the planets are in orbit around the sun. When a planet travels around the sun, one year has passed on the planet. Some planets have short years. Some planets have very long years.

②

Solar System Booklet *(cont.)*

The Sun

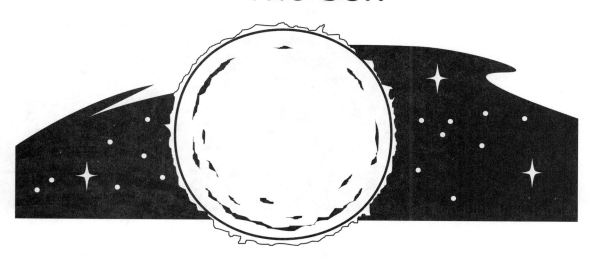

The sun is really a star. It is the closest star to Earth. It is a fiery ball of gas. The sun is important to us. It gives warmth and light to our planet. The sun changes the season and the weather. The nine planets in the solar system revolve around the sun.

③

Mercury

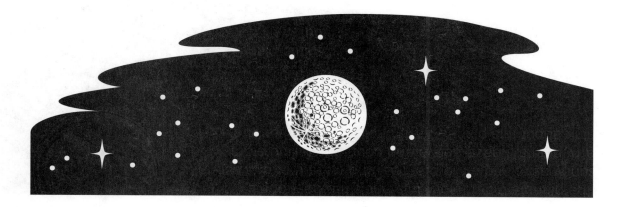

Mercury is the closest planet to the sun. It is the smallest of the inner planets. It does not have any moons. Mercury is covered with craters. It looks a lot like our moon. One side of Mercury is always burning hot and one side is always freezing cold.

④

Solar System Booklet *(cont.)*

Venus

Venus is the second planet from the sun. It has no moons. It is called Earth's twin planet because the two are about the same size. Venus is a very hot planet. It has thick clouds that hold in heat. It rotates in the opposite direction of the other planets. Venus has earthquakes, volcanoes, and loud thundering storms.

⑤

Earth

Earth is the third planet from the sun. It has one moon. It is an amazing planet because it has life. No other planet in the solar system has people, animals, and plants.

⑥

32

Solar System Booklet *(cont.)*

Mars

Mars is the fourth planet from the sun. It has two moons. It is called
The Red Planet because of its color. It is much smaller than Earth.
Mars has seasons that are similar to Earth's.

⑦

Jupiter

Jupiter is called the King of Planets. It is the largest planet and is the
fifth from the sun. Jupiter is covered with colorful clouds. This planet
has four large moons and many other small moons. It has rings like
Saturn, but they are not easily seen.

⑧

Solar System Booklet *(cont.)*

Saturn

Saturn is the sixth planet from the sun. It is yellow and gray in color. The only planet larger than Saturn is Jupiter. It is known for its rings. Saturn has more than 20 moons!

Uranus

Uranus is the seventh planet from the sun. It has a bluish-green color. Uranus has rings and five large moons. Uranus spins on its side. Scientists think that it was hit by a large object and tipped over.

34

Solar System Booklet *(cont.)*

Neptune

Neptune is the eighth planet from the sun. It also has rings. It is blue in color. Neptune has a spot called the Great Dark Spot. It is really a large storm. Neptune has eight moons.

Pluto

Pluto is the smallest planet. It is the ninth and farthest planet from the sun, so it is covered with ice. Pluto has one moon that is almost its size.

Research Outline

Name of planet: _____

Location of the planet: _____

Planet's color: _____

Fascinating facts: _____

_____

_____

_____

_____

Your opinion: _____

_____

_____

_____

Illustration of the planet:

Experiments

Directions from the Sun

Your students will be interested to know that a watch and the sun can act as a compass.

Materials: an analog clock, analog watches

Directions:

1. Take students outside with an analog wall clock.
2. Aim the hour hand of the clock in the direction of the sun.
3. The area halfway between the hour hand and the twelve will indicate south.
4. Use several other clocks or watches to see if south can be located at different times of day.

Solar Shadows

Allow your students to experiment with shadows with this activity.

Materials: tagboard, empty juice cans

Directions:

1. On a sunny day, take students outside, armed with sheets of tagboard and empty juice cans.
2. Have each student prop up his or her tagboard and use the juice can to make different shadows on the tagboard.
3. Encourage the students to move the can to make a cylindrical shade, a circular shadow, etc. What happens when the tagboard is placed in different areas or directions?
4. Encourage the students to discuss their findings.

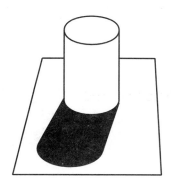

What Makes a Day?

Help your students to understand day and night with this demonstration.

Materials: a free-standing globe, a flashlight

Directions:

1. Place a globe on a tabletop and turn off the lights in the classroom.
2. Shine a flashlight on the globe and explain to the students that the sun shining on a portion of the earth causes daytime.
3. Draw students' attention to the dark side of the globe. What time of day is it on that side of the world?
4. Select a student to hold the flashlight aimed at the globe. Slowly turn the globe to show how the earth rotates throughout the day. As the earth turns, different parts of the world experience daytime and nighttime hours.

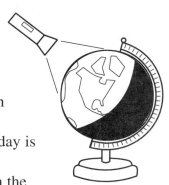

Make a Shadow Clock

Before there were clocks, people used shadow clocks or sundials to tell time. To make a shadow clock, follow the directions below.

Materials

- shadow clock triangle pattern (page 39)
- pencil
- two sheets of tagboard
- glue or tape
- pins or small nails

Directions

1. Cut out the triangle pattern and trace it onto tagboard. Then, cut out the tagboard triangle.

2. Fold along the solid line, and crease one tab to the right and one to the left.

3. Attach the tabs of the triangle to the center of the remaining tagboard sheet using glue or tape.

4. Take the shadow clock outside, shortly before noon, with a pencil and some pins or small nails.

5. Find a place on the ground where the shadow clock will not be disturbed. Position the clock so that there is no shadow to the sides of the triangle when it is exactly noon.

6. Secure the clock in place by pressing pins or small nails through the bottom tagboard sheet into the ground.

7. Check the shadow clock every hour on the hour and mark with a pencil where the shadow falls. Continue in this manner through the school day and again the following morning.

8. On each day, have the students check the shadow clock to tell the time. Encourage them to compare this clock to a watch for accuracy.

Make a Shadow Clock *(cont.)*

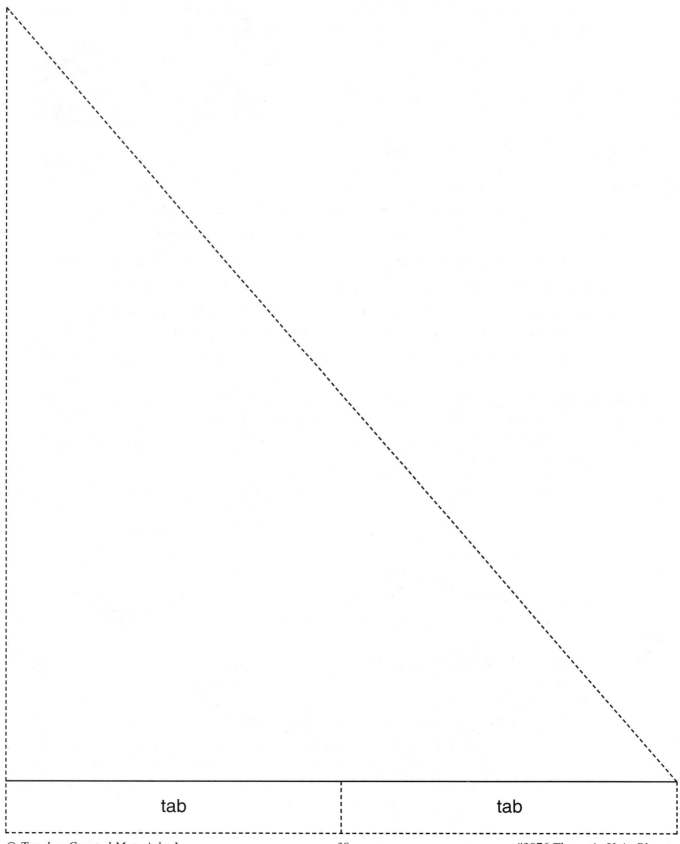

tab   tab

Moon Landing

On July 2, 1969, history was made when Apollo II took Neil Armstrong and Edwin Aldrin ("Buzz" Aldrin) on a journey to the moon. They landed after five days of travel and were the first men to set foot on the moon's surface. The world watched as the men stepped from the craft and heard Armstrong's words, "That's one small step for man, one giant leap for mankind."

The astronauts collected samples of moon rock and soil. They took photographs, performed experiments, and set up equipment that would be used to send information back to Earth. This great event led to several more lunar orbits and opened the door to space travel and study of the solar system.

Peek-a-boo Rocket Book

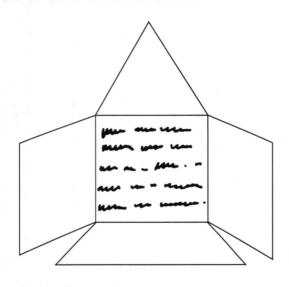

Have students demonstrate their knowledge of the first moon landing by creating peek-a-boo rocket books. To make a book, each student needs a copy of pages 41 and 42. Have students cut out the patterns. Glue the rocket top and bottom onto the center piece on the tabs and allow the glue to dry. On the lines provided, ask students to write about the historic moon-landing event. Then fold and crease on the dashed lines. Students may color the rockets, as desired, to complete their projects.

Moon Rocks

Your students can make their own moon rocks with an easy-to-make dough. To make the dough, mix together the following ingredients:

- 4 cups (960 mL) flour
- 2 cups (480 mL) salt
- 2 cups (480 mL) water

- 1 cup (240 mL) dry tea leaves (new or used)
- silver glitter (optional)
- waxed paper

Knead the ingredients until the dough is smooth and pliable. If the dough is too dry, add a bit more water. If the dough is too sticky, add a bit more flour. Add a few sprinkles of silver glitter, if desired. Have each student mold a small portion of dough into an interesting rock shape. Allow the rocks to dry on waxed paper for several days. Display them with the peek-a-boo rocket book described above.

Moon Landing *(cont.)*

See page 40 for directions.

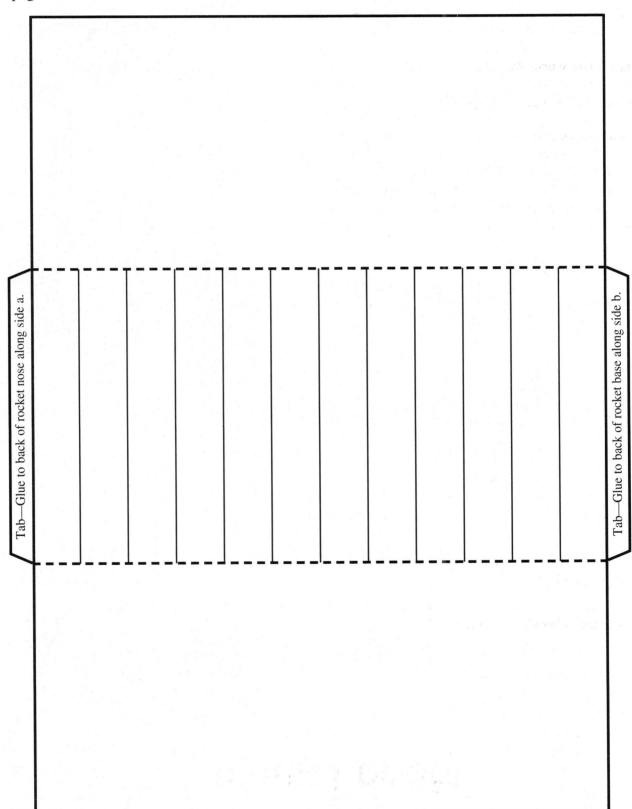

Tab—Glue to back of rocket nose along side a.

Tab—Glue to back of rocket base along side b.

Moon Landing *(cont.)*

See page 40 for directions.

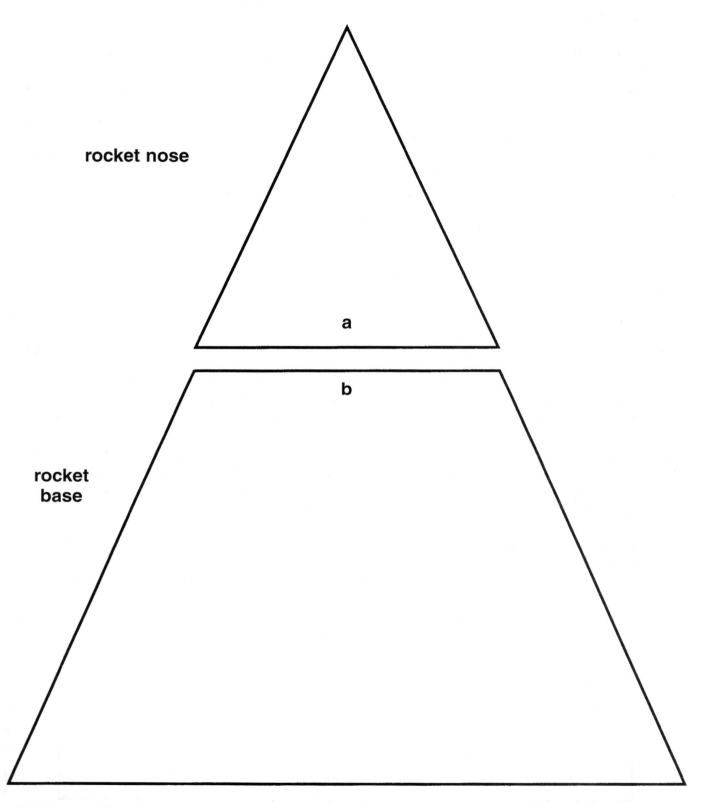

rocket nose

a

b

rocket base

Voyager Space Probes

The twin *Voyager* spacecrafts are like robots that carry their own power, propulsion, communications systems, and scientific instruments. They were designed to travel to the outer reaches of the solar system, and from 1977 to 1989, they transmitted information that greatly increased scientists' knowledge about space, as well as about Jupiter, Saturn, Uranus, and Neptune.

The *Voyagers* are controlled by a set of electronic brains. The spacecrafts can correct their course on their own. If necessary, the electronic brains can be reprogrammed in flight to respond to changing conditions.

A radio antenna is used to send messages to Earth. This tiny radio is able to transmit information over great distances which can be received on Earth.

One of the more interesting features of the *Voyager* spacecrafts is the recorded greeting from Earth that is intended to communicate a story of our world to alien life forms. Each *Voyager* carries a specially-made phonograph record that contains sounds and images selected to illustrate life and culture on Earth. Each record provides instruction in symbols that explain the origin of the spacecraft and how to play the record.

In 1979, eighteen months after launch, *Voyager 1* reached Jupiter, while *Voyager 2* followed four months later. Pictures of Jupiter and its moons were sent to Earth with great detail. Both spacecrafts sent information and photographs of Saturn in 1981 revealing images of a seventh ring around the planet. After the Saturn flyby, *Voyager 1* continued on its journey to the edge of the solar system. Meanwhile, *Voyager 2* flew by Uranus in January, 1986, and told scientists that it had ten moons not previously known. *Voyager 2*'s encounter with Neptune in August, 1989, surprised scientists by showing that the planet had a large, hurricane-like storm, similar to Jupiter's Great Red Spot. This led scientists to call the new discovery the Great Dark Spot.

As they make their way to the edge of the universe, the spacecrafts continue to return information about space. The cameras on board have been turned off, but as long as the spacecrafts travel, several other instruments will continue to send information back to Earth. Scientists expect the *Voyagers* to function for another 20 to 30 years.

Discussion Questions

- How many *Voyager* spacecrafts are there?
- What controls these spacecrafts?
- What is on board the *Voyager* spacecrafts?
- Why is there a record on the *Voyagers*?
- What planets have the *Voyagers* passed by?
- How are the *Voyagers* able to send information to Earth?

Voyager Mini-Booklet

My *Voyager* Mini-Book

1

The *Voyagers* are two spacecrafts. They were sent into space to learn about planets in our solar system. They have been in space for more than 20 years.

2

In 1979, the *Voyagers* took pictures of volcanoes on Jupiter's moons.

3

The *Voyagers* flew by the planet Saturn. They took many pictures of it. People thought Saturn had six rings. The pictures showed seven rings. *Voyager 1* flew farther out in space.

4

44

Voyager Mini-Booklet *(cont.)*

Voyager 2 showed scientists ten new moons around the planet called Uranus.

5

When *Voyager 2* flew by Neptune, scientists learned that it has many storms. There is a very big storm on Neptune that is like a hurricane. It is called the Great Dark Spot.

6

Both Voyagers are now flying farther into space. They do not send pictures back to Earth anymore. They still send important information about space.

7

How much do you remember? Answer the questions.

1. What are the *Voyagers*?

   _____

   _____

2. What did the *Voyagers* see on Jupiter's moons?

   _____

3. How many rings did the *Voyagers* see around Saturn?

   _____

4. What did scientists call the big storm on Neptune?

   _____

8

How Much Do You Weigh?

Gravity gives objects weight. Gravity is different on each of the planets. Your weight would change if you visited another planet because of the gravity.

Use the chart below to answer the questions.

Weight of a 60-pound Child

Planet	Weight (in Earth pounds)	Planet	Weight (in Earth pounds)
Mercury	23 pounds	Saturn	64 pounds
Venus	4 pounds	Uranus	54 pounds
Earth	60 pounds	Neptune	68 pounds
Mars	23 pounds	Pluto	4 pounds
Jupiter	152 pounds		

1. On which planets would you weigh the least? _____

2. On which planet would you weigh the most? _____

3. Would you be heavier on Saturn or Venus? _____

4. Would you be heavier on Neptune or Mercury? _____

5. Which planet has the most gravity? _____

6. Write the names of the planets in order having the least gravity to the most.

_____

_____

_____

Interesting fact: If a 60-pound child visited the moon, he or she would weigh about 10 pounds!

Is Pluto a Planet?

The planet Pluto was discovered by a man named Clyde Tombaugh in 1930. Its moon, Charon, was discovered in 1978. It is the most distant planet that has been found in our solar system. However, there has been much controversy about Pluto in recent years. Is it really a planet or is it an asteroid?

What is an asteroid? Webster's dictionary describes an asteroid as "one of many small planets between Mars and Jupiter with diameters from a fraction of a mile to nearly 500 miles." Many scientists say that asteroids are small and irregularly shaped. They were also formed by particles coming together, which is why they are unusually shaped. A planet, on the other hand, is typically described as being round and orbiting a star.

Pluto orbits a star, our sun, every 248 years. It is a round body that is about 1,429 miles (2300 km) wide. It is, by far, the smallest planet in our solar system. Even Mercury is more than double its size. Although Pluto is much smaller than any of the other planets, it is more like Earth than Jupiter or Saturn. Pluto and Earth have solid surfaces, while Jupiter and Saturn are made of gas.

The decision was made on February 3, 1999, by the International Astronomical Union that Pluto will continue to be classified as a planet. But what do you think? Is Pluto a planet or an asteroid?

Activities

1. As a class, make a comparison chart to compare an asteroid to a planet. Remember that asteroids are described as being irregularly shaped, having a width of 500 miles (800 km) or less, and orbiting a star. Planets are described as being round and orbiting a star. Should Pluto be classified as an asteroid or a planet?

2. Why the controversy? If Pluto meets the criteria of a planet, why was there any controversy in the first place? Engage your students in a discussion of this topic.

3. Have students work in pairs to create posters advertising Pluto as either a planet or an asteroid. Encourage students to talk with their peers in other classes to share their opinions and gain support for their beliefs.

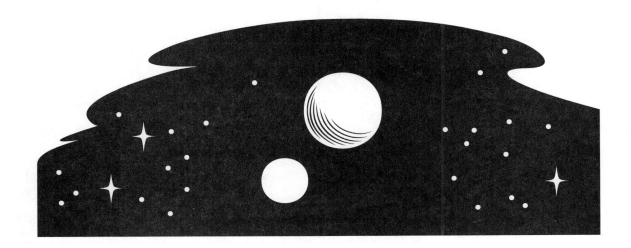

It's in the Stars

Use a pushpin to make a hole through each dot. Then attach the page to a window to see the constellations shine.

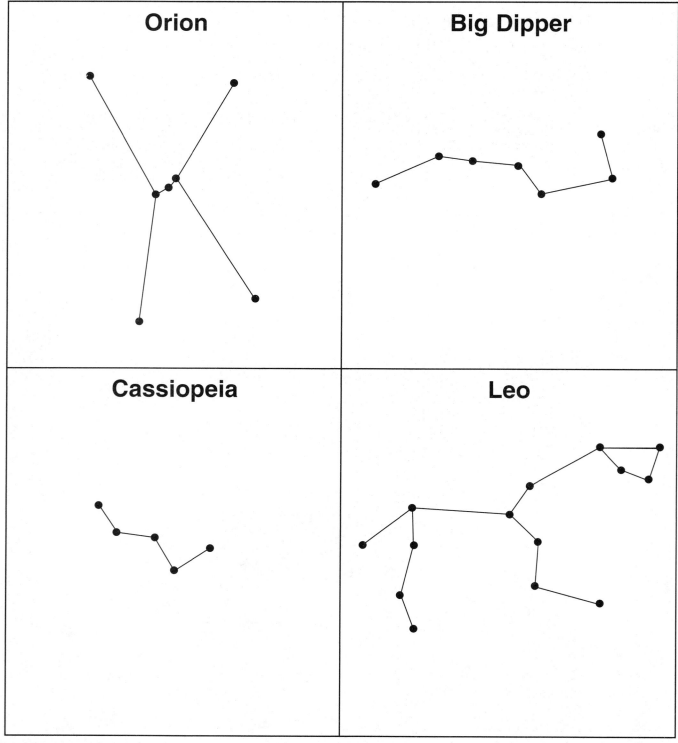

Now, try to find these constellations in the night sky.

Race to the Sun

Directions

1. Draw a card and read the fact.

2. Read the number in the corner of the card.

3. Move that number of spaces.

4. The first person to reach Finish (the sun) wins.

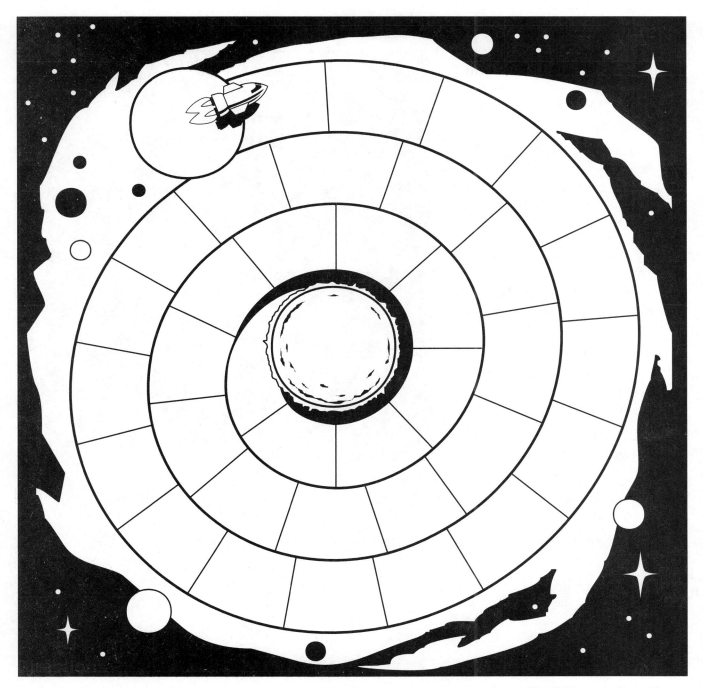

The Milky Way Galaxy

With this project, show your students just how small our solar system really is within our galaxy.

Materials

- one sheet of 9" x 13" (23 cm x 33 cm) black construction paper
- blue, yellow, and white chalk (broken into one-inch pieces)
- red crayon
- aerosol hairspray

Directions

1. Explain to the students that our solar system is located within a huge galaxy called the Milky Way. There are many other galaxies in the universe.

2. To create a galaxy, begin by laying the blue chalk on its side and rubbing it in the center of the construction paper to make a circle. Then, keeping the chalk on its side, make a swirl pattern extending out from the circle. This can be done by swirling once from the bottom of the circle and once from the top (as shown).

3. Using the yellow chalk, rub atop the blue chalk from the center to about halfway out on the swirl lines.

4. Finally, use the white chalk to rub over about half of the yellow markings.

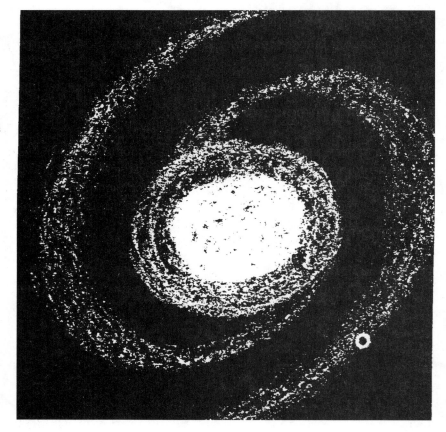

5. To indicate our solar system within the galaxy, use the red crayon to make a small dot toward the outer portion of the swirl lines.

6. To prevent the project from smearing, lightly spray it with hairspray and allow it to dry. (**Note:** Have an adult spray the paper away from the class and in a well-ventilated area.)

7. Label the project, "The Milky Way Galaxy," using white chalk.

Miniature Solar System

With this project, students can make colorful solar system models.

Materials

- one 2-inch (5 cm) Styrofoam ball
- yellow or orange marker
- pencil
- glue (if needed)
- salt dough (See recipe below.)
- toothpicks
- tempera paints (assorted colors)
- paintbrush
- waxed paper
- square Styrofoam base (optional)

Directions

1. Use the marker to color the Styrofoam ball. This will represent the sun.

2. Push the eraser end of the pencil into the ball. Secure with glue, if necessary.

3. Use the salt dough mixture to make nine balls in varying sizes. Press a toothpick into each ball and allow to dry overnight.

4. Paint each ball to resemble a different planet. Allow to dry on waxed paper.

5. Next, attach the planets to the sun by pushing the toothpicks into the Styrofoam ball.

6. The completed project can be used as a pencil topper or pressed into a large, square piece of Styrofoam to make a base for the free-standing project.

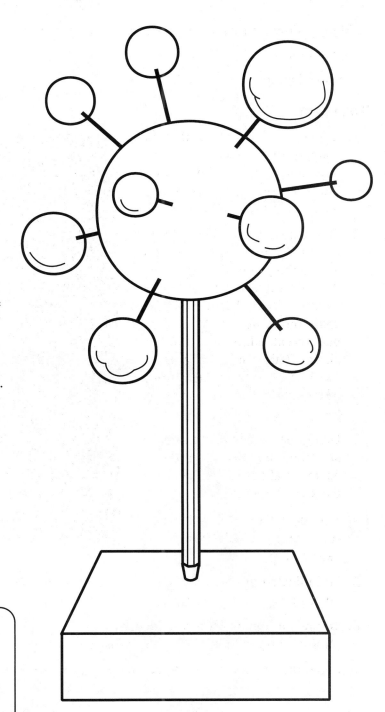

Salt Dough Recipe

Mix 1 cup (250mL) salt,
2 cups (500 mL) flour, and
1 cup (250mL) water to form a pliable dough.

Magnetosphere

Each planet has a magnetic force. The force is called a magnetosphere. A magnetosphere is the space surrounding a planet that acts like a barrier to the planet. Earth has a magnetosphere, too. You can visually demonstrate the earth and its surrounding magnetic field with this art project.

Materials

- Earth pattern (enlarged from below)
- markers, crayons, or colored pencils
- 13" x 18" (33 cm x 46 cm) sheet of black construction paper
- glitter (silver and/or gold)
- pencil

Directions

1. Color and cut out the Earth pattern. Glue the earth cutout to the center of the black construction paper.

2. Using a pencil, draw large ovals beginning from the center of the earth and extending beyond (see the illustration for placement).

3. Squeeze a trail of glue along the pencil-drawn lines. Sprinkle glitter onto the glue lines and then shake off the excess. Allow the project to dry before displaying.

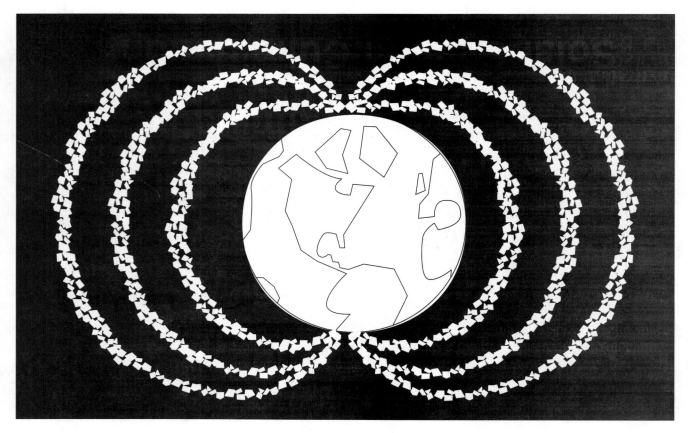

Stars in a Box

Your students can enjoy a night sky anytime of day with this project.

Materials

- one copy of the cube pattern (page 54)
- black construction paper
- pencil
- a pushpin
- tape or glue
- scissors

Directions

1. Trace the cube pattern onto black construction paper and cut it out.

2. Use a pushpin to poke numerous holes on all sections of the cutout.

3. Use a pencil to press a peek hole through the center of one of the sections.

4. Assemble the cube by folding in along the dashed lines and taping or gluing the tabs to the appropriate sides.

5. Peer through the peek hole to see the stars.

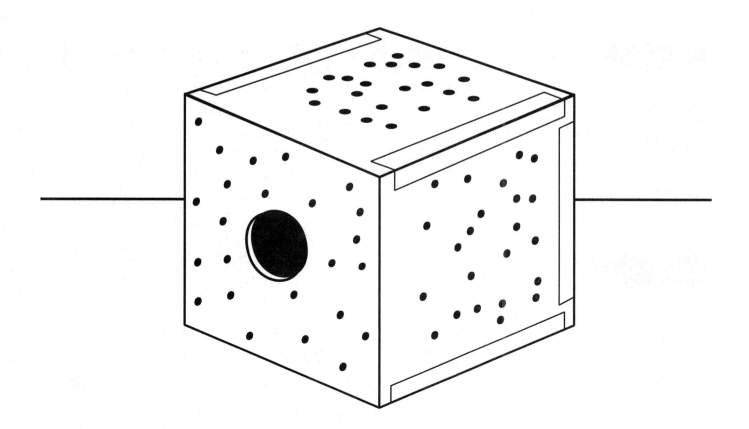

Stars in a Box *(cont.)*

See page 53 for directions.

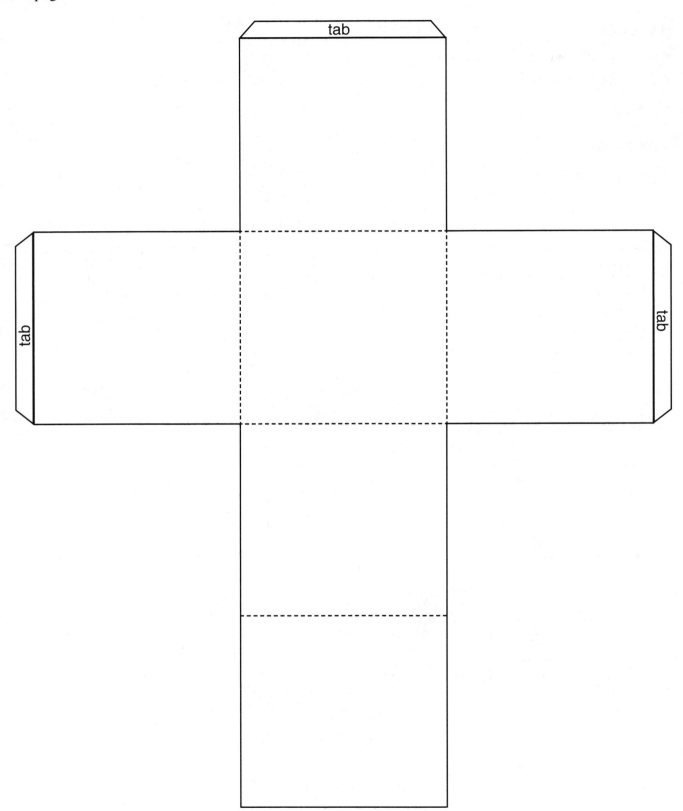

54

Space Creature Pencil Can

Set the mood for the thematic unit by having students adorn their desks with decorative pencil cans.

Materials:

- four 1" x 3" (2.5 cm x 7.6 cm) strips of construction paper
- glue
- one empty soup can (label removed)
- pencil
- crayons or markers
- construction paper (assorted colors)
- scissors

Directions:

1. Accordion fold each of the construction paper strips. Glue the ends of two of the strips to the can for arms. Glue the ends of the remaining two strips to the under side of the can for legs.

2. Using a selected color of construction paper, draw, color, and cut out the space creature's head and glue it to the outside top of the can.

3. Color and cut out other decorative shapes and designs and glue them to the can, as desired.

4. When the glue is dry, place the can on a desk and fill with pencils, markers, scissors, and other useful items.

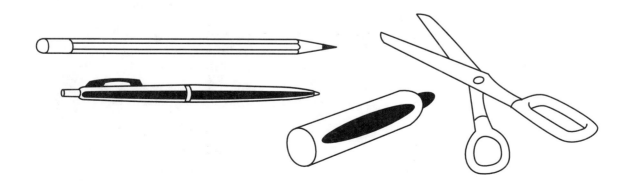

Space Songs

Twinkle, Twinkle, Great Big Star
(Sung to the tune of "Twinkle, Twinkle, Little Star")

Twinkle, Twinkle, great big star,
Shine upon us from afar.
All the planets that are found,
Traveling around and around.
Twinkle, twinkle, great big star,
Shine upon us from afar.

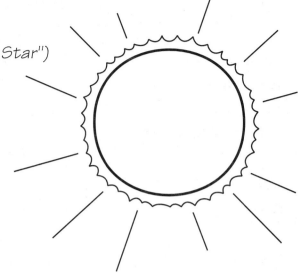

The Sun's a Fancy Clock
(Sung to the tune of "Hickory, Dickory, Dock")

Hickory, dickory, dock,
The sun's a fancy clock.
The shadow's stray throughout the day,
Hickory, dickory, dock.

Earth is our Planet
(Sung to the tune of "You Are My Sunshine")

Earth is our planet, amazing planet,
It orbits 'round and 'round the sun.
It gives us food and refreshing water,
And lovely sunsets when day is done.
We love our planet, amazing planet,
It gives warmth and rain and air.
Let's all be good to our lovely planet,
For it is left within our care.

Out-of-This-World Treats

Milky Way Cookie

Create out-of-this-world galaxy cookies with this recipe.

What You Need

- plastic knife
- chocolate frosting
- one three-inch round sugar cookie

- waxed paper
- galaxy pattern (shown)
- sprinkles
- small round candy
- scissors

Directions

1. Use the plastic knife to ice a sugar cookie with chocolate frosting.

2. Using a pair of clean scissors, cut from waxed paper the swirl design (see illustration).

3. Place the waxed paper cutout atop the iced cookie. Then shake on light-colored sprinkles. (You may choose a light-colored icing and dark sprinkles, instead.) Gently remove the waxed paper and discard it.

4. Show the location of our solar system in the Milky Way Galaxy by pressing a small round candy near the outer edge of the cookies.

Solar System Cookie

These treats allow students to create edible solar systems.

What You Need

- plastic knife
- frosting
- one three-inch round sugar cookie
- ten round candies in a variety of colors and sizes

Directions

1. Use the plastic knife to ice the sugar cookie with a desired flavor of frosting.

2. Select a large round candy to place in the center of the cookie to represent the sun.

3. Then position nine other candies, in varying sizes, around the sun to represent the planets.

(**Note:** Check with parents regarding food allergies their children may have. Make appropriate substitutions.)

Out-of-This-World Games

Sun, May We?

Take the students outside to a large open space for this solar system game. Have them stand in a large staggered circle and select one student to stand in the center of the circle as the sun. In turn, each student asks the sun a question, such as, "Sun, may we rotate two times?" or "Sun, may we orbit three times?" The sun responds by saying, "Yes, you may," or "No, but you may rotate/orbit one time." The students then turn in a circle (rotate) or move around the sun completely (orbit) that number of times. Periodically, select another student to stand in the center as the sun.

Star, Star, Planet!

This game is a version of Duck, Duck, Goose. Have the students sit in a circle in a large open area. Select one student to be "it." The student who is "it" walks around the outside of the circle, gently tapping classmates' heads, saying, "Star, star, star, star, Neptune!" When the student names a planet, the student tapped runs around the circle after the student who is "it." If the "it" student is tagged before reaching a space to sit down, he or she remains "it." If he or she sits before being tagged, the other student is "it." Continue in this manner (with the "it" student naming a different planet) until all the students have had the chance to participate.

Asteroid Tag

Here's a version of Freeze Tag that your students are sure to enjoy. Play this game in a large open space. Select three students to be asteroids and one student to be the sun. The remaining students will be planets. To play, the asteroids try to tag the planets. If a planet is tagged, he or she must "freeze" until touched by the sun. Then he or she is free to run again. The asteroids try to "freeze" all of the planets and the sun tries to "unfreeze" them. The sun can also be "frozen," but only by two asteroids at the same time. Continue play in this manner, changing the roles of the asteroids, sun, and planets periodically.

Are You a Planet Expert?

Write true or false beside each sentence. Check your answers to see if you're a planet expert.

_____ 1. Saturn is larger than Mercury.

_____ 2. Jupiter is the largest planet.

_____ 3. Earth is the second planet from the sun.

_____ 4. Pluto is the closest planet to the sun.

_____ 5. Venus is one of the outer planets.

_____ 6. Neptune has rings.

_____ 7. Uranus is tilted on its side.

_____ 8. Mars has life.

_____ 9. Venus is a hot planet.

_____ 10. Mars is one of the inner planets.

_____ 11. Saturn has no moons.

_____ 12. The sun is a star.

_____ 13. There are six planets in our solar system.

_____ 14. The planets orbit the sun.

How many questions did you answer correctly?

12–14 You're a planet expert!

8–11 You're on your way!

1–7 You're a beginner. Keep trying!

Solar System Culmination

Enjoy one or all of these activities to culminate your student's learning experiences. Invite friends to share in this out-of-this-world good time!

❏ **Invitations**

Invite parents, administrators, and/or students from other classes to join you in your culminating experiences. Duplicate and cut out the invitation on page 61. Color and fold the invitation and add appropriate details to the inside (date, time, location) and deliver the completed invitations.

❏ **Programs**

Duplicate, cut out, and decorate the program on page 61. Have students distribute programs to guests as they arrive. Remind guests to write a check mark beside each activity as it is completed.

❏ **Story Sharing**

Have the students share *Louis and the Night Sky*, *Postcards from Pluto*, and other planet and solar system books with the guests. Invite the students to use their puppet props (page 15) to retell *Postcards from Pluto*.

❏ **Art Projects**

Have the students show guests the following art projects:

- The Milky Way Galaxy (page 50)
- Miniature Solar System (page 51)
- Magnetosphere (page 52)
- Stars in a Box (pages 53 and 54)
- Space Creature Pencil Can (page 55)

❏ **Science Activities**

Invite guests to participate in the following space experiments and demonstrations:

- Solar System Booklets (pages 30–35)
- Planet Research (page 36)
- Directions from the Sun (page 37)
- Solar Shadows (page 37)
- What Makes a Day? (page 37)
- Make a Shadow Clock (pages 38 and 39)
- Peek-a-boo Rocket Books (pages 40–42)
- Moon Rocks (page 40)
- Voyager Mini-Booklets (pages 44 and 45)

❏ **Games**

Play the following space games:
- Sun, May We? (page 58)
- Star, Star, Planet! (page 58)
- Asteroid Tag (page 58)

❏ **Songs and Poems**

Have the students sing Space Songs (pages 56) and recite Planetary Poetry (pages 18 and 19).

❏ **Treats**

Serve your guests Milky Way Cookies and Solar System Cookies (page 57).

Solar System Culmination *(cont.)*

Invitation

Join Us for an Out-of-This-World Experience!

Date: _____

Time: _____

Place: _____

_____

Program

Out-of-This-World Experience

Schedule of Events

After experiencing each activity below, place a check mark beside it.

❏ Listen to space stories.

❏ Look at art projects.

❏ Look at space projects or try an experiment.

❏ Play a game.

❏ Listen to songs and poems.

❏ Enjoy delicious treats.

Have a Heavenly Time!

Bulletin Board Ideas

Our Sensational Solar System

To create the background for this display, place a sheet of black bulletin board paper on the floor and squeeze dots of glue in random places on the paper. Then sprinkle silver glitter atop the glue and allow the glue to dry. Shake off excess glitter and then attach the paper to a bulletin board. Duplicate, color, and cut out the planet clip art on pages 70–72. (For large bulletin board displays, enlarge patterns.) Staple the planets to the board, as shown.

Stellar Stories

Display students' creative writing on this eye-catching display. Design the background by using black or dark blue bulletin board paper with a light-colored or star-design border. Cut out large star shapes and have each student write a story on a star. Decorate the stars as desired, and staple them to the board. Encourage students to read their classmates' stories.

The Planetarium

A designated corner of your room can be transformed into a planetarium learning environment that can serve as an intriguing reward for your students.

Creating the Planetarium

Designate a corner of your room for your planetarium area. Position bookcases or dividers to create a mini-room. Leave a space for a small entrance (see Entering the Planetarium below). Cover the top of the mini-room with black bulletin board paper. Use a tack to poke small holes all over the paper. (These will look like stars from inside the planetarium.)

Add to the Planetarium

- Posters, Internet photos, or magazines cutouts of planets, moons, constellations, comets, and asteroids
- Books about planets, the solar system, and space exploration
- Index cards with planet facts attached to the walls
- Suspended spheres to represent planets
- A flashlight
- Any other desired planet-related materials or games
- A sign-in sheet and a pencil attached to a clipboard

Entering the Planetarium

The Planetarium can be set up as a free-time or planned center area, a reading corner, or as an incentive for students' good behavior. For use as a behavior incentive, duplicate and cut apart the planet coupons and chart on page 64. Distribute the planet coupons to students who exhibit positive behavior or good citizenship. Each time a student receives a coupon, it is glued to his or her chart. When a predetermined number of spaces on the chart have been filled, the student gets to enter the planetarium for a designated amount of time.

When a student enters the planetarium, he or she signs in and then spends time browsing through the information and materials inside. When the student is ready to leave the planetarium, he or she signs out. At the end of each day, check the sign-in sheet to see which students were visitors. Invite the visitors to share their experiences in the planetarium and tell about the things they learned.

The Planetarium (cont.)

Planetarium Coupons and Coupon Chart

Name _____

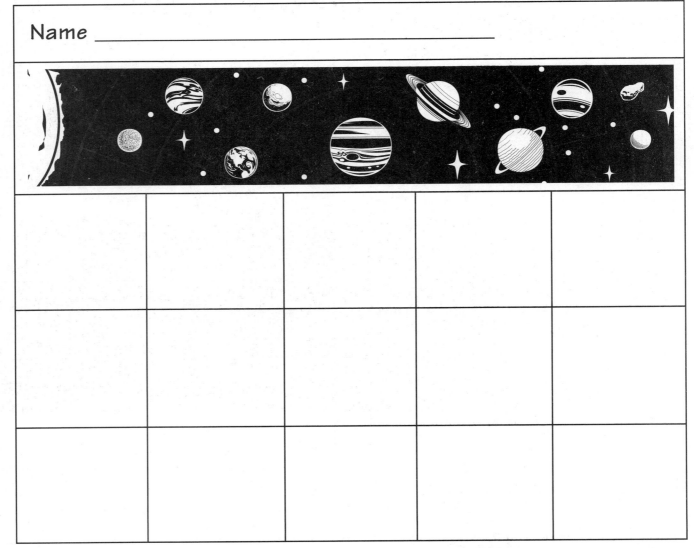

64

Making a Big Book

Big Books are a wonderful language arts experience that combines reading, writing, speaking, and listening, and encourages artistic creativity.

Directions:

1. Before making the Big Books, gather all of the students into one group and review the names, order, and characteristics of the planets and interesting facts they have learned. Brainstorm or review a list of vocabulary words that might be useful when writing the Big Books, such as solar system, space, orbit, rotation, and galaxy.

2. Provide each student or cooperative group (group size should not exceed four students) with six large sheets of black or dark blue paper (at least 12" x 18" [30 cm x 46 cm]). One sheet will serve as the book's cover. The students may write a title on the cover first or choose to wait until the remainder of their book is completed.

3. On each of the remaining five sheets (pages), the students feature one particular planet per page (using the front and back of each page). Information learned about the nine planets is written at the bottom of each page (either in white crayon or on an attached white piece of paper) and a colored clip art illustration (pages 70–72) of each planet is glued above the written information. (Have younger students dictate information to an adult who in turn can write the shared information on each page.)

4. Have the students or an adult hole punch and stack the completed pages in correct sequence (title page followed by the planets pages). Push brads (brass fasteners) through the hole punches to secure the pages.

5. Encourage the students to read their planetary fact books to one another. If desired, have the students share their Big Books with other students during library time or by visiting other students' classrooms.

Cards for Spacey Stories

Use with the Spacey Stories daily writing activity on page 21.

the red monster	the spotted creature
the first astronaut	my little sister
the three martians	my family
the day the spaceship	the babysitter
the biggest asteroid	the second-grade class
the creaking noise	the first time I
the outer space explosion	the creature from Pluto
the smallest alien	my pet

66

Cards for Spacey Stories *(cont.)*

Use with the Spacey Stories daily writing activity on page 21.

on the moon	traveled around the sun
went to Jupiter	and the cosmic vacation
visited Earth	and the space map
lost in space	visited Uranus
traveled to Saturn	flew to the moon
and the telescope	contacts Mars
and the mysterious sound	had breakfast on Jupiter
and the lost shoe	and the flying saucer

Race to the Sun Cards

Use with the Race to the Sun Game on page 49. Use the extra cards for other planet facts that you would like to include in the game.

The path of a planet around the sun is called an orbit. (1)	Venus has strong storms. (3)	Uranus has rings. (1)	Pluto is covered with ice. (3)
There are many other solar systems in space. (2)	Venus has canyons, mountains, and volcanoes. (4)	Uranus has 15 moons. (2)	Venus spins backwards from the other planets. (4)
The inner planets are Mercury, Venus, Earth, and Mars. (3)	Mars has two moons. (1)	Neptune has rings. (3)	Mars has a reddish color. (1)
The outer planets are Jupiter, Saturn, Uranus, Neptune, and Pluto. (4)	Summer days on Mars are freezing cold. (2)	Neptune has bluish-green clouds. (4)	Mars has volcanoes and canyons. (2)
Mercury and Venus are the only planets without moons. (1)	Jupiter has a large red spot. This spot is a big storm. (3)	Neptune has a dark spot like Jupiter. It is a spin-ning storm cloud. (1)	Jupiter is made of gas. It does not have hard ground like Earth. (3)
The sun is a star. (2)	Jupiter has 16 moons. (4)	Neptune has eight moons. (2)	Saturn has 18 moons. (4)
Earth is the third planet from the sun. (3)	Saturn is a large planet, but it is not heavy. It could float on water. (1)	It took 12 years for a spaceship to reach Neptune. (3)	(1)
Earth has one moon. (4)	Saturn has rings made of rocks, ice, and dust. (2)	Pluto was the last planet that scientists found. (4)	(2)
Earth is the only planet with air and water. (1)	Uranus is covered with green clouds. (3)	Pluto and its moon are almost the same size. (1)	(3)
It takes the earth 365 days to orbit the sun. (2)	Uranus is tilted on its side. (4)	There may be other planets in our solar system. (2)	(4)

68

Star Stationery

Clip Art

Earth

Mars

Venus

Mercury

Clip Art *(cont.)*

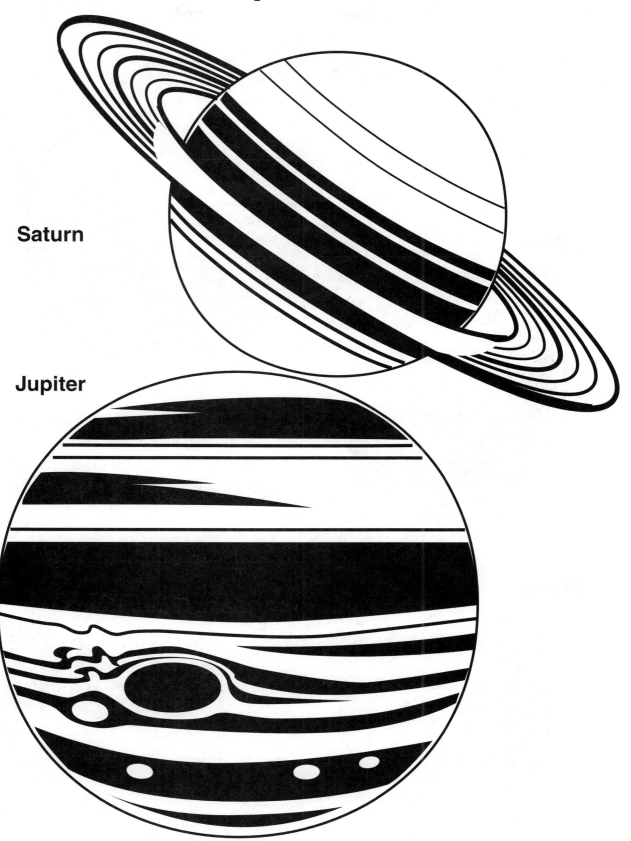

Saturn

Jupiter

Clip Art *(cont.)*

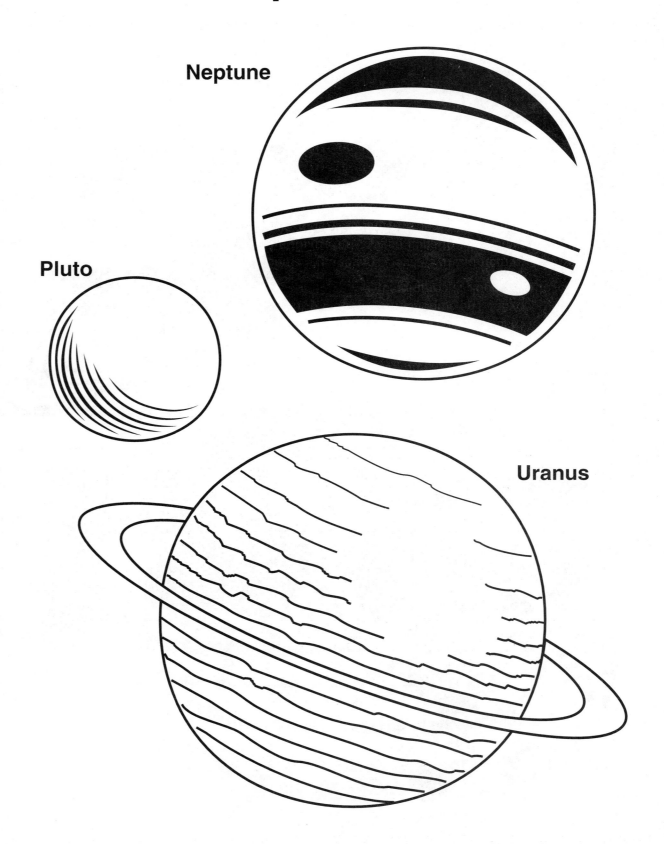

Neptune

Pluto

Uranus

72

Awards

_____ is

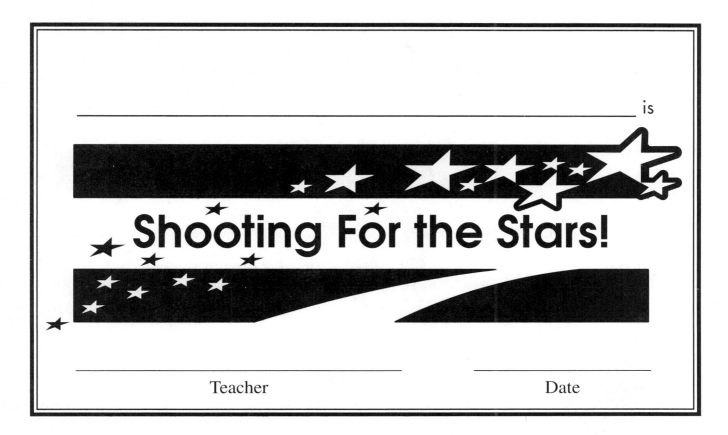

_____   _____
Teacher   Date

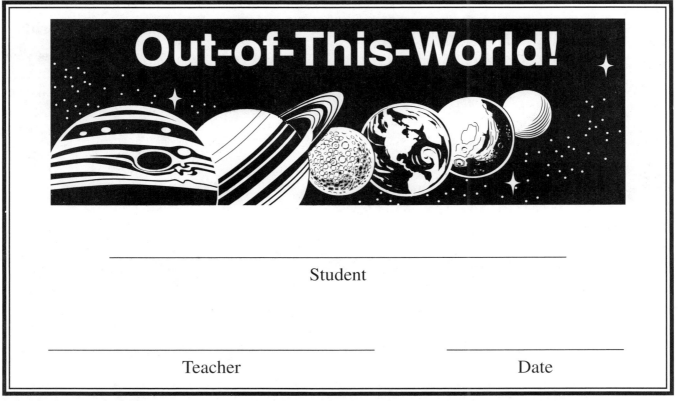

_____
Student

_____   _____
Teacher   Date

Planetary Web Sites

Site 1—Kindergarten Planets

For basic research about planets, this is the site to visit. Students can find basic information about each of the nine planets.

Site 2—Maps of the Solar System

While learning about the planets in our solar system, students will enjoy seeing up close photographs of the planets' surfaces. Click on a planet image to bring up a new and interesting view.

Site 3—NASA's Planetary Photojournal

This Web site not only has dazzling photographs of the planets, but also provides a wealth of scientific information about them.

Site 4—The Nine Planets Glossary

The extensive glossary of planetary terms at this Web site is a great teacher resource for this thematic unit.

Site 5—Planetary Science Spacecraft

This site provides photographs and information about spacecraft used to bring images of the planets back to Earth.

Site 6—Seeing the Solar System

High-powered telescopes are often used to view outer space, but this site provides information about how to see planets using the naked eye as well as binoculars.

Site 7—Solar Eclipse Index

Access this site to view engaging photographs of solar eclipses.

Site 8—The Solar System

Students will be immediately drawn to the beautiful planetary images at this Web site. To use the site, a student simply clicks on a planet image and more photos and information appears.

Site 9—Virtual Solar System

Here's another Web site with stunning photographs of each of the nine planets and the sun.

Site 10—Views of the Solar System

At this Web site, you'll find photographs of planets and information about planets, comets, asteroids, space exploration, and much more. You can also access videos that will fascinate students.

Site 11—Welcome to the Planets

View a collection of NASA's planetary exploration images at this site. You'll also find a glossary of terms and links to many other planetary Web sites.

Site 12—Your Weight on Other Worlds

What's your weight on other planets? At this Web site, a student enters his or her current weight and immediately learns how that weight would change on other planets.

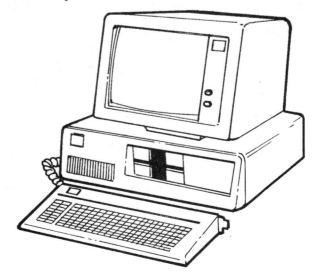

Web Site Activity Sheet

Connect to The Space Place Web site at http://spaceplace.jpl.nasa.gov/spacepl.htm for fun activities. Complete this page to explain your experience.

1. Make a space project and write about it below.

_____

_____

_____

_____

_____

2. Play a game, complete a puzzle, or solve a riddle. Write about it below.

_____

_____

_____

_____

_____

3. Do a space activity and write about it.

_____

_____

_____

_____

_____

Web Site Activity Sheet *(cont.)*

4. Learn space facts. Write about three facts below.

_____

_____

_____

_____

_____

_____

_____

_____

5. Look at student drawings and writings. Write about your favorite one.

_____

_____

_____

_____

_____

_____

_____

_____

_____

Bibliography

Fiction

Carbin, Eddie. *Arty the Part-Time Astronaut.* 3 Pounds Press, 2000.

Coffelt, Nancy. *Dogs in Space.* Harcourt Brace & Company, 1993.

Cole, Joanna. *The Magic School Bus Lost in the Solar System.* Scholastic Trade, 1992.

Cole, Norma. *Blast-Off!: A Space Counting Book.* Charlesbridge Publishing, 1994.

Ingoglia, Gina. *Amanda Visits the Planets.* Inchworm, 1998.

Nonfiction

Beasant, Pam. *1000 Facts About Space.* Kingfisher Books, 1992.

Berger, Melvin. *Do Stars Have Points?: Questions and Answers About Stars and Planets.* Scholastic Reference, 1999.

Boiurgeois, Plauetter. *The Moon (Starting with Space Series).* Kids Can Press, 1997.

Branley, Franklyn. *The Planets in Our Solar System.* Econo-Clad Books, 1999.

Branley, Franklyn Mansfield. *The Moon Seems to Change (Let's-Read-and-Find-Out Science Book).* HarperTrophy, 1987.

Daily, Robert. *Earth (First Books—The Solar System Series).* Franklin Watts, 1996.

Fowler, Allan. *The Sun's Family of Planets (Rookie Read-About Science).* Students' Press, 1992.

Goodman, Susan. *Amazing Spacefacts: Solar System, Stars, Space Travel.* Peter Bedrick Books, 1993.

Greeley, Ronald. *The NASA Atlas of the Solar System.* Cambridge University Press, 1996.

Jackson, Kim. *Planets.* Econo-Clad Books, 1999.

Kerrod, Robin. *The Night Sky (Let's Investigate Science).* Marshall Cavendish Cor., 1996.

Kerrod, Robin. *The Students' Space Atlas: A Voyage of Discovery for Young Astronauts.* Millbrook Press, 1992.

Ridpath, Ian. *Stars & Planets Atlas (Facts on Files).* Checkmark Books, 1993.

Simon, Seymour. *Jupiter.* William Morrow & Company, 1988.

Simon, Seymour. *Mars.* Mulberry Books, 1990.

Bibliography *(cont.)*

Nonfiction *(cont.)*

Simon, Seymour. *Mercury.* Mulberry Books, 1998.

Simon, Seymour. *Neptune.* Mulberry Books, 1997.

Simon, Seymour. *Our Solar System.* William Morrow & Company, 1992.

Simon, Seymour. *Saturn.* William Morrow & Company, 1998.

Simon, Seymour. *Uranus.* William Morrow & Company, 1987.

Simon, Seymour. *Venus.* Mulberry Books, 1998.

Sorensen, Lynda. *Comets and Meteors (The Solar System).* The Rourke Book Company, Inc., 1993.

Vogt, Gregory L. *Asteroids, Comets, and Meteors.* Millbrook Press, 1996.

Weissman, Paul. *The Great Voyager Adventure.* J. Messner, 1990.

Software

3-D Tour of the Solar System

This CD-ROM program of planetary images is suitable for Macintosh or PC.

Lunar and Planetary Institute. Order number: C-ATLAS. Call 1-800-801-9895 or for more information visit their Web site at http://cass.jsc.nasa.gov/education/products/3d_flyer.html

Slides

The Solar System in 3-D

This set of three-dimensional slides comes with one pair of 3-D glasses.

Lunar and Planetary Institute. Order number: S-SOLAR. Call 1-800-801-9895 or for more information visit their Web site at http://cass.jsc.nasa.gov/education/products/3d_flyer.html

Answer Key

Page 9

Louis couldn't fall asleep.

Louis looked at the night sky.

He traveled past Venus.

Louis traveled past Pluto.

He saw a twinkling planet in the sky.

Louis came home and went to sleep.

Page 10

1. Mercury
2. Venus
3. Mars
4. Answers will vary.
5. Answers will vary.
6. Uranus
7. Neptune
8. Answers will vary.

Page 17

Page 22

1. The King of Planets
2. The Red Planet
3. Earth's Twin
4. The Big Blue Marble
5. The Ringed Planet
6. The Double Planet

Page 23

Answers will vary.

Page 26

Neptune

2, 6, 3

5, 4, 7, 1

Pluto

13, 18

16, 14, 11

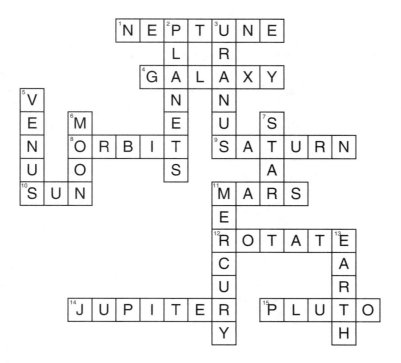

Answer Key *(cont.)*

Page 27

1. Earth, Mars, Jupiter, Saturn, Uranus, Neptune, Pluto
2. Earth
3. Jupiter, Saturn, Uranus, Neptune
4. Mercury, Venus, Earth, Mars
5. Jupiter, Saturn, Uranus, Neptune, Pluto

Page 28

1. Jupiter
2. Venus
3. Mars
4. longer
5. longer
6. Earth

Page 29

1. Answers will vary.
2. 330 years
3. 744 years
4. 24 years old
5. 336 years old
6. Mars
7. Mercury and Venus

Page 45

1. The *Voyagers* are two spacecrafts.
2. volcanoes
3. seven rings
4. The Great Dark Spot

Page 46

1. Venus and Pluto
2. Jupiter
3. Saturn
4. Neptune
5. Jupiter
6. Pluto/Venus, Mercury/Mars, Uranus, Earth, Saturn, Neptune, Jupiter

Page 59

1. true
2. true
3. false
4. false
5. false
6. true
7. true
8. false
9. true
10. true
11. false
12. true
13. false
14. true